In a Class

of Your Own

Own

D1617205

To my dear mother and father.

In a Class
of Your Own

Essential Strategies for the New K–6 Teacher

Rhoda M. Samkoff

CORWIN
A SAGE Company

For information:

Corwin
A SAGE Company
2455 Teller Road
Thousand Oaks, California 91320
(800) 233-9936
Fax: (800) 417-2466
www.corwin.com

SAGE Pvt. Ltd.
B 1/I 1 Mohan Cooperative
    Industrial Area
Mathura Road,
    New Delhi 110 044
India

SAGE Ltd.
1 Oliver's Yard
55 City Road
London EC1Y 1SP
United Kingdom

SAGE Asia-Pacific Pte. Ltd.
33 Pekin Street #02-01
Far East Square
Singapore 048763

Printed in the United States of America

Library of Congress Cataloging-in-Publication Data

Samkoff, Rhoda M.
    In a class of your own : essential strategies for the new K-6 teacher / Rhoda M. Samkoff.
        p. cm.
Includes bibliographical references and index.
ISBN 978-1-4129-8667-0 (pbk.)
    1. Elementary school teaching—United States. 2. Education, Elementary—
United States. I. Title.

LB1555.S16 2010
372.1102—dc22   2010011332

This book is printed on acid-free paper.

10   11   12   13   14   10   9   8   7   6   5   4   3   2   1

Acquisitions Editor:	Hudson Perigo
Associate Editor:	Joanna Coelho
Editorial Assistant:	Allison Scott
Production Editor:	Veronica Stapleton
Copy Editor:	Adam Dunham
Typesetter:	C&M Digitals (P) Ltd.
Proofreader:	Gretchen Treadwell
Indexer:	Sheila Bodell
Cover Designer:	Scott Van Atta

Contents

Preface   vii

Acknowledgments   ix

About the Author   xi

Introduction   1

1. Preparing   3
   You Are Not Alone   3
   Taking Care of Yourself Before Taking Care of Others   4
   Keeping Your Sense of Humor   6
   Defining Your Role as Teacher   6
   Work Relationships   8
   Community Connections   9

2. Anticipating   11
   Strategies for Preventing Common Mistakes   11
   Frequently Asked Questions   14

3. Organizing   19
   Efficient Storage and Retrieval Systems   19
   Purposeful Projects   21
   Using Teaching Space Wisely   22
   Health and Safety First   22

4. Managing   27
   Keys to Managing Groups   27
   Exercise and Productivity   28
   Planning   29
   Handling Paperwork   29
   Behavior Issues and Disciplinary Options   30

5. **Communicating**   **35**
Miscommunication Happens   35
Meeting the Parents   37
The Parent Conference   38

6. **Instructing**   **39**
Formulating Clear Objectives and a Plan   39
Differentiating Instruction   40
Review, Review, Review . . .   42
Motivating   42
"Take Out Your Homework"   44

7. **Observing and Being Observed**   **47**
Be Yourself . . . and Be Prepared   47
Learning by Observing   48

8. **Respecting**   **51**
Providing for Differences and Disabilities   51
Cultural Diversity and Your English Language Learners   52
Teaching Values   54

9. **Reflecting**   **59**
Self-Assessment: A Sign of Professional Growth   59

References and Additional Resources   **63**

Index   **65**

Preface

Ironically, a teacher's early years in the profession are marked, not by teaching, but by *learning*. Unraveling the complexities of the classroom can be a lengthy and sometimes confounding process.

In a Class of Your Own: Essential Strategies for the New K–6 Teacher responds to the need for a practical and upbeat guide for novice teachers. It is straightforward and encouraging in its approach. This book offers a tripod of support, humor, and wisdom that clarifies the process, addresses concerns, and offers strategies for dealing with common situations. It is written in the voice of a mentor who "neither lectures nor judges."

This book also provides easy retrieval of information on a wide range of topics, such as strategies for planning effective lessons, communicating with parents, observing and being observed, and dealing with specific student behaviors. Advice from experienced teachers is supported by examples and anecdotes from the author's classroom. T.I.P.S, the author's acronym for Theory-Into-Practice Strategies, can be found in each of the nine chapters: Preparing, Anticipating, Organizing, Managing, Communicating, Instructing, Observing and Being Observed, Respecting, and Reflecting.

Building skills and enthusiasm are at the heart of *In a Class of Your Own: Essential Strategies for the New K–6 Teacher* and make this book a valuable instructional resource.

Notes

Acknowledgments

I have many knowledgeable people to thank for the development of this book. My sister, Karen, planted the idea, and she watched over it when it took root. After that, the book grew quickly like the kidney beans on the windowsill of my classroom.

This book thrived on the encouragement of friends and family, colleagues and administrators, especially Richard L. Brodow, EdD, and from experienced teachers Evelyn Giventer and Judith Schades. It burst into bloom with wonderful recollections from Carol and Jacklyn Chapman, Larry Dantus, Lynn Reandeau, Ann Stone, and Edward Warshow.

By sharing their expertise, Arthur Fredman; William Gaventa, MDiv; Lawrence Giventer, PhD; Ron Goetzel, PhD; Harold Klein; Jory and Lahsen Oulhiad; Dimitriy Vyacheslavovich Plotnikov, PhD; Aron Samkoff; and *The Wordmaster* gave the book strength and depth. The expert editorial staff at Corwin, especially Hudson Perigo, Allison Scott, and Veronica Stapleton gave it a dignified place in the academic garden.

If this book is a plant that has grown out of constant and tender care by so many, then to my students past and present I humbly say thank you, as you are the flowers that flourish from its messages and show your beautiful selves to the world.

PUBLISHER'S ACKNOWLEDGMENTS

Corwin and the author gratefully acknowledge the contributions of the following reviewers:

Jane Ching Fung
Kindergarten Teacher/Mentor

Alexander Science Center School
Los Angeles, CA

Patricia Palmer
Sixth-Grade Teacher
Wynford School
Bucyrus, OH

Leslie Standerfer
Principal
Estrella Foothills High School
Goodyear, AZ

Cathern Wildey
Adjunct Professor of Education
Retired HS English Teacher
Holiday, FL

About the Author

Rhoda M. Samkoff is a teacher in the Millburn, New Jersey school system. She holds a master's degree in curriculum and teaching from Teachers College, Columbia University in New York City, and is a member of Kappa Delta Pi International Honor Society In Education. Ms. Samkoff has taught at all of the elementary-school grade levels. More than 70 of her students have received honors or awards in writing competitions or have had their work published. She is also the advisor of a leading elementary school student council that has received nine national awards of excellence, including a United States Congressional Certificate of Recognition.

Ms. Samkoff has mentored student teachers and new teachers and has instructed in the Education Department at Kean University in New Jersey. She has presented workshops and seminars in successful teaching techniques and authored numerous articles that have appeared in educational magazines and in the *New York Times*. Ms. Samkoff has received awards for innovations in education, writing, and student leadership, and is a 2010 Teacher of Honor.

Introduction

Teaching is a wordy business . . . millions of words have been used to explain the history, philosophies, pedagogy, and methodologies of teaching, but working with young students requires additional, practical skills that you acquire only through experience.

Since the beginning, survival has depended on teaching and apprenticeship. From building shelters to building cities, from making adaptations to making new discoveries, human existence relies on our ability to educate the next generation.

There is an art, a rhythm, a virtual trapeze of pacing, timing, anticipation, planning, decision making, and self-control. You are not alone in wondering if you have the expertise or the safety net to deal with the minute-to-minute needs of a group of children.

This book puts into your hands the skills that you need to become an effective teacher right from the start. T.I.P.S., or Theory-Into-Practice Strategies, is an acronym frequently used in this book. These will give you useful ways to sharpen those tools. In the reassuring voice of a mentor who neither lectures nor judges, this book offers you wisdom and witticism for a successful start.

WHAT IS TEACHING?

Teaching is like taking a kayak out on the river. You soon discover that no two days are exactly the same. Some days, the river is calm. Things go smoothly, and you can enjoy the natural rhythm and flow.

On other days, you may need to call upon your skills to navigate tricky rocks and rapids. You become keenly aware of the clues around you: gathering clouds, an increase in wind, and a drop in temperature. In the same way, teachers watch the "barometer" for changes in

1

their classrooms. You, too, will learn to recognize the verbal and nonverbal cues that give teachers valuable information about how to proceed.

Experienced travelers never carry extra baggage because time and practice have taught them to focus on the essentials. In a similar way, the efficient use of time and materials is another important aspect of teaching.

Just as there is a haze on the river, and you cannot see what is ahead, teachers are often challenged by students who do not understand. Those who have been there say, "Be patient. The haze will lift." How true this is for both teachers and students.

We know that the cycle will continue. The river will be there next summer, as will the birches and the mountains. One after another, groups of children will pass through your care on their scholastic journeys.

If we do our best to strengthen their confidence and academic foundation, to help children appreciate beauty and respect one another, then we are an essential part of the cycle, and can be assured that we are performing our jobs well.

But satisfaction is fleeting. Even before we can begin to miss the first, a new batch of students arrives. There is always one more child to nurture, one more strategy to try, one more goal to reach.

Teaching is, and always will be, an endless process filled with changes and challenges. However, if you stay as energized and optimistic as you are at this moment, you will not only experience success, but you will also collect precious memories along the way.

Today may the waters speak to you of rich adventure and dreams yet to be discovered.

—*Native American Proverb*

CHAPTER ONE

Preparing

YOU ARE NOT ALONE

All teachers have one important thing in common: We all started out as students, with none of the responsibilities for planning or instructing. Then, one day, we found ourselves on the other side of the desk. As one novice teacher told me, "I went from attending the show to running it!"

One of my colleagues looks back at her first year of teaching this way: "After *that* milestone, I realized that teachers share something special regardless of our length of service, size of school, the grade level, or the department. Teachers feel an instant bond when we meet anywhere for the first time."

It's a rare novice who doesn't experience some nervousness along with anticipation, so I suggest that you review this list:

Eleven General Principles of Teaching

1. Birthdays and lost teeth are more important to a child than the addition facts.

2. A student who feels respected, accepted, and safe is apt to become successful.

3. Teaching is not about control: Good teaching is about good management of external conditions. *Lead, guide, assist, manage, motivate, demonstrate,* and *respect* are key words when working in the field of education.

4. Teaching is not about the teacher. Students need to be reassured that every day is a new day, and that their mistakes or misbehavior have been forgiven or forgotten.

5. There is simply no room in the classroom for embarrassment or anger. Every child should go home at the end of the day thinking, "My teacher likes me."

6. Teaching takes energy. (Can you handle the physical rigors?)

7. Teaching takes patience. (Are you willing to wait, repeat, and listen to others?)

8. Teaching requires creativity and flexibility. (Do you enjoy the challenge of coming up with new ideas or changing existing ones to fit new situations?)

9. Teaching requires accountability and reflection. (Are you willing to accept suggestions and take responsibility for your actions?)

10. Teaching takes acceptance and understanding. (Do you understand the stages of child development and the assortment of behaviors that accompany them?)

11. Teaching requires interpersonal skills. (Are you comfortable and effective in front of a group? Do you respect individual differences?)

If you have answered yes to these questions, then don't just stand there outside the classroom door . . . Come in! Come in!

TAKING CARE OF YOURSELF BEFORE TAKING CARE OF OTHERS

Read the materials and curriculum guides supplied by your school district, and familiarize yourself with the policies and procedures. It expedites processing if you have your health records, birth certificate, and proof of certification.

As you go through the year, keep a record of the workshops you attend, with the date, number of hours, title, and presenter. At some point, you may be asked to document your professional development. Also, save your yearly contracts. You will be busy, but when you look back you'll be glad that you updated your resume or curriculum vitae (CV) regularly with regard to committee work, awards and professional conferences, publications, and other accomplishments.

T.I.P.S

A person who returns calls and messages promptly, completes forms accurately, and treats people courteously is perceived as organized, competent, and confident. Step off to successful teaching by keeping a record with the information on this sheet.

Information Sheet

Teaching start date: _____

School address: _____

Name of district: _____

Principal: _____

Secretary: _____

Supervisor: _____   Telephone: _____

Mentor: _____   Telephone: _____

Substitute call-in telephone: _____ (if applicable)

School hours: _____ to _____

Grade-level assignment: _____

Superintendent of schools: _____

Preparing also involves thinking ahead and finding materials, such as pictures and articles, that can spark writing and discussions. Now is also a good time to start a list of people who would be willing to make presentations to your class.

One of my colleagues strongly advises keeping up with your calendar. Plan ahead for events, such as school-colors days, back-to-school night, conference days, luncheons or special lunch days, assemblies, and field trips.

She learned the hard way, showing up at school on the day of a field trip to the Bronx Zoo—wearing heels and a white linen suit.

Do you have a special interest or skill? Take stock of your own talents. There may be opportunities for you to teach a class or coach a sport before or after school.

KEEPING YOUR SENSE OF HUMOR

A quick check in the morning helps prevent embarrassing moments. I recall the day the principal came into a classroom sporting a new, bright green top with the size sticker still stuck in the middle of her ample chest. "Mrs. W," one of the little girls spelled out loudly and proudly, "you're L-A-R-G-E—large!"

Not only will children notice everything, from the tiny bandage on your elbow to your toe ring, but they will also ask you why it's there, and where you got it. They don't ask questions to embarrass you or to be rude: *they just want to know.* When one teacher walked into her room with a new, shorter haircut, she was greeted by a hushed class until somebody called out, "Ms. B, you got your haircut!" which was immediately followed by, "We liked it better the other way."

Spontaneity is what makes teaching so unique. One child calls you "mom." Another unclenches his fist and offers you a bunch of half-melted chocolate covered raisins. Children cry sometimes and giggle sometimes and sneeze all over the place. Oh, and they step on your shoes.

One afternoon, I pulled up a chair next to a kindergartener, so I could help him with a gluing activity. We both ended up sticky, so I suggested that we wash our hands. "I don't need to," he replied as he wiped his hands all along the arm of my new striped sweater. "I'll just use this towel."

DEFINING YOUR ROLE AS TEACHER

Defining your role as a teacher can be accomplished in four ways. Perform routine tasks without complaining. Show sincere thanks or appreciation to groups or individuals who give you help. Apologize for mistakes without offering excuses, and show confidence without arrogance.

We can all take a lesson from the young pair-skating duo that was trying out for the Olympic team. The TV commentator was silent for the entire four minutes of their flawless program. Then he said, "These two skaters have been skating together for only two years. The reason they're strong contenders is because they are aggressive on the ice . . . and they never apologize for their lack of experience!"

A novice has *plenty* to offer. Just think about it. You're fresh and motivated. You may be able to see teaching applications for new technology. You're eager to try out new ideas and methods, and every day is an opportunity to learn, and experiment, and find out what works for you.

Remember, you're only a neophyte until the next one comes along. My first principal told me that another teacher was scheduled to start in March, and asked me to show her the ropes. So just like that, after only three months, I was no longer a newbie.

T.I.P.S.

Don't assume that you have complete anonymity when you are off duty. Even if you live in a different neighborhood, city, or town from the one in which you teach, you may be recognized. Because of your connection to the school, the likelihood that you'll be spotted by many other students and their families increases. Although many students are savvy, it's interesting that some of the very young children still find it hard to imagine that their teacher has a life away from school. Even the older ones show a little surprise and embarrassment when our lives collide with theirs in places like the pizzeria or the mall.

Of course, when you are away from school, the time is yours to go out and do as you please; but don't be surprised if, on Monday, a student says, "We (or my parents) saw you at _____ on Saturday." The blank can be completed with any one of the actual *teacher sightings* that follow, so it's a good idea to be conscious of and careful about what you are saying or doing in public:

I saw my teacher . . . in a restaurant, at a movie theater, a tennis match, or a department store, at a car wash, a bank, casino, or hair salon, at the local Fourth of July fireworks, at the dentist, at an airport, in a laundromat, at a political rally, on a ski lift . . . or at the police station.

WORK RELATIONSHIPS

An elementary school is a unique workplace filled with small furniture and books with happy endings. We go to "school" in the morning, rather than to "work." You'll find school symbols, mottos, school songs, and mission statements designed to boost positive social interaction.

In many ways, teachers are dependent on one another, whether it's the teacher next door who covers your class for a few minutes or the art teacher who loans you paint brushes when you run short. Although your family and friends may be there for you, your colleagues are the ones who are truly able to commiserate with you. I've never encountered a teacher who refused to give advice to a novice who needed it.

It has been said that the style and the personality of the principal sets the tone for the school. Some principals request that their teachers resolve classroom issues, while others prefer to be informed of the details and handle problems themselves.

Some principals like to work directly with students and are visible and approachable during the day while others spend more time with administrative duties. Still others strike a balance. But regardless of the style of your ship's captain, the "big three" for teachers are being *prompt, prepared,* and *proactive.* Hand in forms, report-card comments for approval, plan books, and other information when due. Be on time for work and meetings, and respond quickly to requests.

Make sure that your plans are up to date. You can anticipate situations by keeping running records and notes on students whom you think may have issues that will need attention. If possible, have discussions with a child's previous teacher, and check information on new students. It's also wise, after a reasonable amount of time, to make the parents aware of any concerns you may have.

Art Fredman, university field supervisor, Kean University, New Jersey, offers additional advice for working cooperatively with your principal or supervisor: "Strive for a good attendance record. Focus on the job ahead of you, and put personalities aside. Respect the position and the experience even though you may disagree with your supervisor. Don't hesitate to ask questions or ask for clarification. Accept suggestions, and try to incorporate the advice by the time of the supervisor's next visit."

COMMUNITY CONNECTIONS

Teachers should be knowledgeable about the municipality in which the school is located. Municipal officials can be a valuable source of information. They can also help guide you in the development of a project involving your students.

—*Harold M. Klein, Executive Director, Downtown Millburn Development Alliance, Millburn, NJ*

T.I.P.S

The following are suggestions for making a positive connection to the community in which you teach:

- Find out the street names in the neighborhood.
- Have your students make a poster of the pictures and names of local government officials.
- Read the local newspaper for events that involve the school, such as elections, town or city clean-up campaigns, ethnic parades or block parties, fundraisers . . .
- Visit local businesses. Many owners support school activities.
- Find out about student groups, tutors, student council, sports teams, and afterschool activities.
- Participate in school and community activities; volunteer to judge an art contest, help out at an event, or attend a student art show or musical performance.
- Consider preparing a display on an educational theme for the local library or for a store window.
- Write about a successful class activity, and submit the press release to the school newspaper if your school has one. You might also submit to a district or interschool newsletter, local paper, or teacher's magazine. (But remember, you must receive written photo permission from students' parents before publishing photographs of your students.)

Notes

CHAPTER TWO

Anticipating

Mistakes: Some are preventable. Others are inevitable. Most are regrettable. No matter how competent and careful you are, there will be blunders, errors, mishaps, and slips. You'll find that many mistakes occur as a result of rushing. For example, a teacher I know wrote a short note to a parent in the moments before dismissal. Her note came back not only answered, but also with the teacher's spelling mistakes circled in red.

I always try to be well-organized for parent conferences. Some years back, a parent asked to see her daughter's standardized test results. I produced the sheet quickly, placed it on the table between us, and smoothed it out. When I saw the parent frown, I glanced at the national percentages and said, "These numbers seem low for Sarah."

"They ought to," the mother answered coolly, pointing to the name on the top of the sheet, "That's not my daughter."

STRATEGIES FOR PREVENTING COMMON MISTAKES

Forgetting to deliver a message to a student: Do it right, and do it right away. Pay close attention to all messages, and act on them immediately.

T.I.P.S.

Children and adults tend to forget messages, even important ones, by the end of a busy school day. In addition to a verbal reminder, you can tape a note to the student's desk or refer to a daily reminder board before dismissal. (Example: Frank: *Take the bus home today.*) Even if the student is out of the room when the message arrives, you've addressed the situation at the time the message required your attention.

Allowing students to leave the room: No one should leave without permission from the teacher. Find out if your school has a required system such as a hall pass or sign-out sheet. If not, you can create your own reliable procedure. In either case, always know the whereabouts of every student.

Making errors in grading: Use a straight edge to align the names with the grades.

Deleting grades or information on the computer: Back up all work, and keep a hard copy.

Mispronouncing students' names: Ask the student directly, and make pronunciation notes.

Missing meetings: Keep a calendar, and check it often.

Guessing a child's age, height, or grade level: Avoid guessing, "Are you in the third grade?" Some children are sensitive about being large or small for their age or grade. Instead ask, "How old are you?" or, "What grade are you in?"

Losing a paper: Photocopy class lists to use as checklists for test papers or homework. You can also use the class list for checking off health forms, permission slips, milk money, and homework assignments.

Leaving a paper in the office or elsewhere in the school: Do not use the school machines to photocopy personal material, such as letters, tax information, legal papers, or receipts.

Promising a reward and then forgetting to deliver: Have the surprise ready first. Promising puts pressure on you to remember. Find out the school's policy on providing treats, or use stickers or other small tokens as occasional rewards.

Running out of time when teaching a lesson: Put your plan on the board. When the lesson is in front of you, it's much easier for you and everyone else to follow. An abrupt ending can ruin the best lesson. Set a timer as a signal to wrap up the session, and then stop. If you haven't covered everything that you had planned, don't worry. Sometimes, it's hard to resist the temptation to squeeze information in at the end of the class, but if the last 10 minutes are rushed, the students will not gain anything from it.

Spending too much time on a unit of study: Divide the units into days or weeks so that you can plan instruction and tests accordingly. Make a schedule and stick to it, so you'll have enough days to cover the material. Use tabs to mark the landmark pages in your teacher's manual to stay on track.

Addressing misbehavior: Teach "visitor behavior" and "substitute behavior" to your students early in the year. Children think of the classroom as *their* turf and see visitors as curiosities. Students know that visitors are unfamiliar with the routine and the rules, which gives the students the home-court advantage, especially with substitutes. Teach your students the ways in which they can help.

Being perceived as too friendly or too strict: Keep the line of professionalism distinctly drawn. First, you must accept the fact that young children ask personal questions, often without realizing that they have overstepped the boundaries of propriety. You can make a short general statement such as, "I don't answer questions about my family" (religion, political preference, etc.), or just respond with a simple, "I'm sorry, but that's personal."

Using discipline too strongly at the beginning of the year: This topic is covered in more detail in Chapter 4, under Behavior Issues and Disciplinary Options, but you can start with setting clear expectations and limits. Have an ascending action plan in place to deal with students who test the boundaries. A questioning look or a simple, quiet reminder may be all you need to calm a situation. However, if a behavior repeats, you will need to address it as an individual or group issue.

Playing favorites: It's easy to pay a great deal of attention to students who are pretty, polite, clean, and cooperative. The challenge is to spend an *equal* amount of time with the students who resist your efforts, whose clothes are not always clean, or those who melt into the background. The shy child or the extremely creative one might require an extra measure of patience. Also, listen to yourself. How do you address the children? Do you use terms of endearment with only some of your students?

Waiting until one or more students misbehave before setting things right: This can lead to more serious problems. When the students are working calmly, compliment them to reinforce the group behavior you expect.

A strategy that works well with classes that have behavioral issues is to have students make a large "class compliment" grid. When another adult (lunch supervisor, substitute, principal) gives a compliment to your class, put a sticker in one of the squares. When the chart is completed, give the class a special activity to acknowledge and maintain their good group behavior.

Mistaking misbehavior for teacher error: Thanks to my first mentor, I learned to use the phrase "look inward" often. A myriad of issues can be resolved when teachers examine their own actions first. When there is a long line at the teacher's desk, it is not surprising that some students will start to act up. I suggest limiting or eliminating the need for children to line up to have their work checked, but if you must, try this: Put a list of no more than six names on the board. Conference with those students one at a time while the rest are working independently. Keep the meetings very brief. Repeat the system periodically until you have reviewed the work of all of your students.

FREQUENTLY ASKED QUESTIONS

I receive numerous questions from new teachers stemming from their concerns, and the first thing I encourage them to do is to restate "What if . . . ?" questions clearly and objectively.

FAQ—What if interruptions cut into my teaching time?

ASK—How can I make productive use of time?

There is no such thing as a typical day. Unplanned events happen. A child forgets his lunch, homework, project, costume . . . a new student arrives, another has a bloody nose. Art class is cancelled because there is no substitute.

There may be a fire drill or other emergency. Planned events, on the other hand, include school assemblies, vacations, and teachers' workshop days.

If you take care of the priorities, the rest will fall into place. Remember, your students can read your attitude, so you might want to use events that are not a part of the regular school day to teach your students to be flexible. For example, an assembly can be followed by a writing activity, so your language arts time is not "lost" but instead is even more valuable because it relates to the previous event.

Avoid long lectures. Keep explanations short and to the point. Break the instruction into smaller segments, and provide intervals for questions and practice.

FAQ—What if my principal (or supervisor) and I don't get along?

ASK—How can I establish a good working relationship with my administrators?

A good way to start is to call the school and introduce yourself to the principal or supervisor. Offer to meet with them prior to your starting date. Be respectful, sincere, and open to suggestions.

FAQ—What if I need to take a sick day?

ASK—What is the policy regarding substitutes?

Know the district's procedure in advance. At home, keep the school telephone number, your daily and weekly schedules, and a class list. Always leave enough plans in your classroom for at least three days. Plans, class list, and weekly and daily schedules should be in full view on your desk in school.

FAQ—What if the students don't like me?

ASK—How can I earn the students' respect?

Concentrate on being fair and kind to every child in the class. Your focus should be on your goal: to provide the best instruction possible for each student. Keep your voice and temper under control. Remember, a good teacher is structured, not strict. Practice the rule *compliment in public, correct in private.*

FAQ—What if the class doesn't listen to me? What if I lose control of the class?

ASK—How can I create an environment where the students will be focused on learning?

Busy, involved students usually don't have time to be disruptive. There are many basic classroom-management techniques that you can try, such as making lessons relevant to students, providing opportunities for student participation, moving around the room, changing desk arrangements, varying the pace, and providing breaks. (Chapters 4 and 6 further discuss this and related topics.)

FAQ—What if my supervisor or principal doesn't like my creative lessons?

ASK—What is the best way to introduce new or creative approaches in a traditional school environment?

Tone it down while keeping your eyes open. Is the school tightly bound to the curriculum and testing?

Is it because the principal is unaware and unsure about the success of the method you are using?

Could it be that your principal is uncomfortable with the fact that you have the students eat the pieces of candy after they have sorted and counted them? Consider that the noise might be higher than your colleagues' or principal's comfort level. Try to understand exactly what is raising an eyebrow, and adjust it.

FAQ—What if the students form cliques and are mean to each other?

ASK—How can I create an environment where everyone feels welcome?

Right from the start, give the students ways that they can settle arguments easily. For example:

"I want to go first!" Have the students roll a die or spin a spinner. The highest number takes the first turn.

"He or she always gets the best classroom job!" Create a rotating job chart.

"It's mine! He or she took my _____ (pencil, eraser, book . . .)." Ask students to label their essentials, including boots, umbrellas, lunch containers, jackets, and other personal items.

T.I.P.S.

Create a lost and found for returns at the end of the day. Children are especially adept at sleuthing to identify each other's "stuff"—especially before dismissal!

Establish a class rule: "No valuables in school." Many teachers will tell you stories about irreplaceable objects that children bring to school to show—and sometimes lose.

Sometimes the child doesn't have permission to bring an item from home. Let parents know your policy concerning appropriate and safe show-and-share items. If you determine that it is valuable, label it, alert the parent, and make a mutually acceptable arrangement for its return.

However, if a child brings in a questionable or potentially dangerous object, contact the principal immediately.

FAQ—What if the students won't do their work?

ASK—What would motivate me to learn?

This question is covered in more depth in Chapter 6 (Instructing). However, most students tend to respond positively when the instruction relates to their own experiences.

Notes

CHAPTER THREE

Organizing

EFFICIENT STORAGE AND RETRIEVAL SYSTEMS

Prior to computers, "cut and paste" and "file-save" were the mantras of the organized classroom. Much of the teacher's time was spent locating or creating instructional materials for classes, and the file cabinet was a classroom staple. However, even though numerous teacher Web sites have made the retrieval of worksheets, graphics, templates, research information, and even lesson plans available, a system for managing paperwork is still a necessity for efficiency and accountability.

You have many options for setting up a retrieval system that works for you. Use whatever is available—closets, boxes, stacking crates, and art portfolios. Arrange *teaching materials* by subject, topic, or holiday. *Instructional charts* can be organized by skill or subject. *Student work* with samples for conferences can be filed in folders alphabetically or color coded for multiage or multilevel organization. *Office work,* such as receipts, copies of forms, and memos, can be filed by general topics, such as technology. *Pictures and other graphics* can be grouped by theme or topic, and *worksheets* can be easily retrieved by subject or skill.

Test yourself: if you can locate what you need in less than 60 seconds, you have a well-organized, workable system!

T.I.P.S.

If you store and label materials carefully at the end of the year, it will assure a smooth start for the following school year.

The majority of the suggestions given to me during my first year of teaching by my mentor, Carl, had to do with collecting and saving. "Go and forage, Grasshopper, and you will be set for winter!" he'd say, and "Always, always, keep extras on hand. If you have 20 students, plan for 25."

I began to notice inexpensive items that came in bulk. I frequented garage sales and flea markets for children's games and workbooks and for other items that had possibilities. Librarians and doctors offered me used magazines, and a shoe-store manager saved me so many mountains of shoe boxes for my students' projects that I had to ask him to stop.

However, nothing beats a resourceful teacher with good contacts. There was the sixth-grade science teacher who obtained part of a nose cone of an actual space capsule into which three students squeezed at a time for their silent-reading session. This went on for years until a fire code required its removal. At a school in Vancouver, Canada, I also saw students curled up comfortably to read . . . in an Inuit canoe.

Free and inexpensive materials are all around us. Take a walk around the school. Leaves, seed pods, pine cones, sand, shells, and other natural objects can be used in art projects. Collect enough objects for a class, with an eye on recycling: common objects such as cardboard rolls, corks, buttons, empty plastic containers, and shoeboxes can be reused for projects. Go to teachers' Web sites for free graphics, printables, and lesson-plan ideas. Don't be shy! Ask for product donations from local merchants.

Certain paper place mats and menus have instructional value. Service organizations often have coloring books for children. The post office donated large posters to our school, and the local post of the American Legion offered us flags and booklets about respectful care of the flag. If your school is in need of teaching materials or supplies, ask your principal about contacting schools that have student councils. They can help by holding collections for school and art supplies.

PURPOSEFUL PROJECTS

Children pull together well when working on a project that benefits others. For example, by making cards for young patients in hospitals, collecting clothing or shoes for people in need, working at a food bank, or tackling an environmental issue, children learn that their actions are useful. The National Association of Elementary School Principals (NAESP) is one source that offers excellent resource material and project suggestions.

According to teacher Judith Schades, projects can also provide stability prior to holidays:

> One of the most challenging times to motivate children to learn is before a holiday. Look at the curriculum and see how a project would fit in. Holiday cards that use geometry, line designs, tangrams, and string art keep students tuned in.

Sixth-grade teacher Evelyn Giventer adds that projects can also make research come alive: "Students look forward to working on projects, whether small or large, that relate to their studies."

During their study of colonial America, her sixth graders pieced together material and a field of stars donated by a local flag company. Their handmade American flag was raised for the school at a special ceremony.

Projects provide enrichment for students at more advanced levels that include reusing and researching skills. A group of students in a sixth-grade class traced a six-foot outline map of their state.

They covered it with cancelled postage stamps from home and school envelopes. The students labeled the capital and points of interest, and they used the computer to research the people and events on commemorative stamps. Their work was displayed in the post office for the community and covered by the local paper.

USING SPACE WISELY

Classroom location and availability can change for many reasons.

When there are crowded conditions, teachers may have to share a room.

Basement rooms, offices, multipurpose rooms, and even hall space may be used to accommodate a growing student population. I taught third grade in a small converted library and fifth grade in a portable classroom located less than 60 feet from train tracks.

Your attitude will transfer to the students; so, instead of complaining, work with your students to make the space—regardless of its size—neat, organized, clean, safe, and comfortable.

"Wallpapering," or decorating every inch of wall space, can be distracting for students with or without disabilities. On the other hand, a classroom that is too sparse does not stimulate learning.

HEALTH AND SAFETY FIRST

Our first priority as teachers is to keep our students safe. We would like to think that schools are safe places, but the building and its occupants are subject to emergencies. Your school administrators will explain how to deal with fires, lockdowns, strangers, and other safety issues; so, expect the unexpected, and whenever you are in doubt about how to handle a situation, ask.

T.I.P.S.

Use a common-sense approach to health and safety issues.

- Know how to contact the school office and nurse quickly.
- Locate the nearest exits and practice alternate evacuation routes.

- Keep exits and vents unobstructed.
- Before school starts, check with the nurse about any students who have medical conditions and how these should be handled (asthma, allergies to chocolate, nuts, milk, bee stings, etc.).
- Watch for and report potentially dangerous situations, such as unsteady or broken furniture, sharp corners, windows without childproof bars, and unsafe traffic conditions.
- Explain and post classroom-safety rules, and go over them with your students on the first day of school.
- Be meticulous in checking permission slips for signatures of parent/guardian.

Stephen came to me, standing stiffly and complaining about a pain in his back.

"When did it start?" I asked. Stephen played football after school, and often had sprains and strains.

"This morning. It really hurts, and I can't bend." I could tell that he meant it.

"You'd better have the nurse check it," I said. As Stephen walked toward the door, I called him back.

"This must be a new shirt," I said, while I removed a clear plastic hanger from between his shoulder blades.

Some of the most exciting moments for students involve the arrival of animals, both invited and uninvited. And over the years, I've had an unusual array of visitors fly, walk, or crawl into my classroom.

I can only imagine the stories that were probably embellished at home about the ants in the coat closet, the lice outbreak, the bird that flew in during math, the bee that stung me on my chair, and the ferret that bit me on the cheek during a visit to the arboretum.

At one time, my school district not only allowed animals in the classroom but also encouraged them. An example was a fifth-grade science unit on the food chain. The teachers received plastic containers with holes in the lids, warming lights, packets of grass seed, and a bag of soil. A few days later the school secretary called about a delivery. "Your crickets are here." For weeks, the classroom was filled with the sound of happy crickets chirping as they fed on the grass seed.

The lights gave off a comforting glow in the back of the room. Then came a dreaded call, "Your frogs are here."

One day during my second year of teaching, Kenny and his mother came in carrying a big glass terrarium.

"We thought you and the class would enjoy seeing Kenny's pets," she said as she set the container down on the table. My fifth graders crowded around. Inside were two enormous tarantulas.

"Don't worry, these are *tame*," Kenny added, and started to reel off facts about them. Kenny had never spoken so much or so animatedly, so I let him continue for a few minutes.

"Oh, one last thing," said his mother, as she sprinkled some sand onto the table. "Tarantulas *love* this. See how they think they're in the desert?"

Without warning, Kenny stuck his arm into the terrarium and let the spiders walk onto his hand and up his arm. He lifted them out and they raced across the "desert." Just then one hissed and the other answered by spitting. In an instant, the two were locked in a tight fuzzy embrace. A fight! A few of the children screamed.

Kenny cried, "They'll *kill* each other!" Both Kenny and his mother were helpless. I had to do something quickly before the tangled spider-ball rolled off the table.

I grabbed the terrarium, balanced it on my knee below the table, and swept the ugly mass into it with a ruler. Kenny's mother clamped on the lid. The tarantulas crawled into separate corners and sulked like boxers who had been separated unfairly.

We watched in silence as Kenny and his mother carried the terrarium out of the room. Then, one of the girls said softly, "That was some science lesson." After that, whenever it came to certain animals in the classroom, I never had any problem with saying no.

T.I.P.S.

Use caution and common sense with discipline.

Matthew was bothering the girls again, and his teacher, Christine, felt she was running out of patience. Finally, she sent him out in the hall "for a few minutes." The children immediately settled down. "A few minutes" turned into 30. If a student hadn't asked, "Where's Matthew?" who knows how much longer it would have been until Christine remembered? Luckily for Christine, Matthew was sitting alone in the hall outside the door, but the scare made her realize the seriousness of her action, and she did not repeat it.

T.I.P.S.

Never leave your class unattended.

Never discipline by sending a child out of the room to stay alone.

Never release a child to an adult who comes to the classroom to pick up the child without authorization from the school administrators.

Notes

CHAPTER FOUR

Managing

KEYS TO MANAGING GROUPS

Stand-up comics have it. So do masters of ceremonies, musical conductors, motivational speakers, DJs, and anyone else who needs to keep their audience engaged. The exchange of energy between teachers and students starts with knowing how to use six keys: pace, balance, content, voice, sound, and timing.

Pace is the speed at which you deliver material. Watch your students' reactions to your word choice, body language, and facial expressions. There are times when speaking and demonstrating quickly are effective, but you should also sense when it's best to slow down or simply stop. Students need time to digest what you are asking them to do.

The second key is *balance.* Watch for clues that your students are tiring. Humor, suspense, and surprise are three elements that, when used sparingly, will keep your class interested. Balance sedentary with energetic activities.

Taking an interesting approach to *content* is a third key to classroom management. Consider playwriting and acting as an enrichment activity. Sound effects and simple props make content come alive, and a group of parents or a class of younger students may be an appreciative audience.

Voice is another important key. Vary your pitch and volume. A whisper can be very effective. You don't have to fill every silent moment with teacher talk. Students will be more focused on what you are saying if there are periods when you are quiet.

The fifth key is *sound*. Some teachers use music to lull an active group. A kindergarten teacher I know played a mellow descending scale on the xylophone, and it worked every time. Other teachers have a signal for silence. Shouting, "Be quiet!" is as unnerving as blowing a whistle.

The last key is *timing* your delivery and response. Master the pause and the wait. Consider not only what you teach but *when*. The weather and time of day affect your students' attention and activity levels, and you can also expect a change in attentiveness before and after holidays and vacations. A competent teacher is aware of the external factors that affect learning—and plans for them.

EXERCISE AND PRODUCTIVITY

Dimitriy Plotnikov, an educator and fitness coach, recommends that after 15 minutes of concentrated effort, teachers should give children a break or make a change in their approach to keep the students' attention.

Students of any age should not be required to sit for long periods of time on chairs or cross-legged on the floor without opportunities to stand and stretch.

As a novice teacher, I knew nothing about neurokinetics, brain research, frontal-lobe activity, or lab-rat aerobics. I *did* know that when college students sat through long lectures, we acted out just like children, whispering, shifting positions, and even dozing off.

I tried "stretch breaks" with my students, which morphed into a few minutes of exercise. Larry Dantus, one of the parents, dubbed this "The Samkoff Stretch." The children returned to their work more energized and better focused.

Ron Goetzel (2005), director of the Institute for Health and Productivity Studies at Emory University in Atlanta, Georgia, has conducted numerous studies on the effect of exercise on productivity.

He wrote to me in 2008:

> I support your efforts to get children in school to be more physically active, eat nutritious foods, and in general, lead healthier lifestyles. There is no doubt in my mind that improving children's health and well being will result in their improved school performance and a healthier, more prosperous community. (R. Goetzel, personal communication, August 4, 2008)

Stretch breaks should be monitored. They consist of one or two minutes of energizing movement, not "free time."

The teacher can work with the students to set up rules, such as "Keep hands and feet to yourselves." The light exercises should be low impact, and they can involve moving to music, or tossing sponge balls to partners. Juggle balls, beanbags, and foot sacks are appropriate options for older students, but no one should perform any balancing or endurance activities.

PLANNING

Teachers keep their plans up-to-date not only because in many schools they are checked periodically by the principal, but also because the plan book doubles as a journal that guides instruction. While it might seem easy to "wing it," the truth is that without plans, the hours loom ahead of you. Also, trying to fill in plans later is a tough task. Take the pressure off, sit down for a few minutes during the day or after school, and make sure that your plans are in order.

Plan for the substitute. Prepare a folder with lessons in each subject area for at least three days ahead. Include instructions, worksheets, page numbers, and a weekly schedule that clearly shows times for special classes, lunch, and dismissal. Also include a class list. It's better to have plans in place than to try to call them in when you are not feeling well, leave your class without plans, or worse, go to work while you are sick because you did not leave plans for the substitute!

HANDLING PAPERWORK

A big pile of uncorrected papers or workbooks on a teacher's desk is a telltale sign that the management system needs adjustment. Try to make it a goal to reduce or eliminate papers by the end of each day. One way to accomplish this is to complete one writing project or assignment before going on to the next. If you create a folder for each student who is absent, it will save you time trying to find the papers the student needs. When a pile of papers is growing, hold a "correcting session" and go through everything before the paperwork gets out of control. Remember, the more paperwork you give, the more you have to correct, so vary the format of assignments; for example, students can read their essays aloud rather than submit them to you.

Return students' work, with the exception of papers you are saving to share with parents or post on the bulletin board. You should see, but *do not* have to correct or grade, every paper that crosses your desk. You can initial that you have seen the work or put a sicker or stamp on it.

"Trading papers" can embarrass students. Instead, they can use a pen or colored pencil to self-correct while you go over the answers. The advantage to this method is that the students actively participate and learn by correcting their work with you. You can occasionally distribute an answer key for the students. Afterward, collect papers for another cursory check.

Give careful thought when creating tests. Blanks that are all at the same side of the page are quicker to correct, and percentages are easier to calculate for 20, 25, or 50 items. For essays, develop a checklist or rubric to justify the grade that the student has received.

Keep grading in mind when designing test questions. For example, a clear two-part question is, "List *three* Acts that were placed on the colonists by the British before the Revolutionary War, and tell *why each Act angered the colonists*." On the other hand, an example of a vague question would be "Discuss some causes of the Revolutionary War."

BEHAVIOR ISSUES AND DISCIPLINARY OPTIONS

Small problems can grow, so be aware of them, and let the parents know your concerns. Parents can react defensively to difficulties at school, as in the case of a parent who attempted to defend his troublesome sixth grader by telling the teacher, "You don't understand because you don't have children." Without hesitation my experienced colleague answered, "If that reasoning were true, there wouldn't be any male obstetricians." Then, they proceeded to work out the problem.

Teachers who lack management skills might resort to desperate measures to control a group, such as sarcasm, threats, or bribes. In fact, they may get things done their way out of the students' fear of reprisal or loss of privileges.

It's possible for a strict teacher to command a certain level of control, but effective teaching and learning takes place only when there is mutual respect.

Misbehavior falls into four main categories:

1. Action that is carried out by one student and does not affect anyone else (e.g., refusing to do class work).

2. Action by one student that affects one other student (e.g., taking someone's pencil).

3. Action by one student that instigates group behavior (e.g., one student calling out, and the rest join in).

4. Actions of a group directed at one or more students (e.g., teasing, ignoring, or other types of bullying).

T.I.P.S.

When we consider the possible reasons for misbehavior, we realize that not all require discipline. The child may be:

- tired
- bored
- sick
- incompatible with a partner (or group)
- frustrated with the level of instruction
- unhappy over an incident at home or at school
- hungry
- in need of exercise
- in need of attention
- unable to concentrate for the same length of time as the others
- excited about an event coming up after school
- lonely
- unable to hear or see from his seat
- distracted by noise or activities of the other children
- unable to control her behavior due to a disability
- unaware or unclear about the rules
- "testing" you to see what you will do
- used to getting his way
- unable to keep up with the pace ("lost")

Always keep your temper under control. Like Franklin D. Roosevelt said, "When you get to the end of your rope, tie a knot and hang on" (ThinkExist.com, 1999–2010). When the topic of responding to student behavior comes up, remember that no matter how clear you think you are, some children might still misunderstand your instructions or explanations. The anecdote that follows is a good example.

A new teacher told me that she had gone over her rules in detail, from keeping sneakers tied to walking correctly through the halls, but, sure enough, halfway down the hall she turned and saw that one of her second graders had stepped out of her perfect line. She admitted that she "lost it" and scolded him. The child tried to explain that he had moved out of line to tie his sneakers. He said tearfully, "I don't know which of your rules comes first."

First among appropriate teacher responses is giving the child a chance to explain or apologize. Size up situations quickly and quietly. When it is necessary to speak with a student, keep it short, as reprimanding can easily turn into ranting.

Be aware of how you come across to the child. Sitting down with a student has a calming effect on both of you. Ignore minor mistakes and misbehavior. Often, a child does something accidentally and hopes that you will not notice, such as coming in late. Other times, the situation resolves itself, as in the case of a second grader who had a heated lunchtime argument with a friend. I had time to speak to the girls only briefly, but while I was reading to the students after lunch one reached over, patted my knee, and said, "Don't worry, we made up."

An adept teacher can distract the students by changing the subject. You can separate students by moving desks or groups.

You can record the incident and issue a warning, or take the concern to the principal. Of course, if the child is out of control, call for immediate assistance.

Teacher Responses to Avoid

- Avoid the instinct to overreact.
- Avoid using the child's behavior as an example for the class.
- Avoid using the words *bad* and *inexcusable*. Instead, focus on the behavior. Use words such as *inappropriate* or *unacceptable*.
- Avoid disciplining the entire group for the actions of one.
- Never use any form of physical contact.
- Avoid yelling. Speak in a firm, controlled voice.
- Avoid threatening a student: be clear about what actions will be taken if the behavior does not improve.
- Avoid cornering, or standing over and literally talking down, to a student.
- Do not take sides until you are sure of the facts.
- Avoid using schoolwork or homework as punishment.
- Never send a student to an unattended area.

Students can read a teacher's nonverbal cues, such as disappointment, disbelief, and alarm; so, sometimes it's more effective not to say anything at all. As an example, Charles ignored the rule about not sitting on the desks. He was a large boy who didn't have good coordination. All of a sudden, Charles lost his balance; and as the class and I watched helplessly, he did a complete backflip off the desk and miraculously landed on his feet! He was as shocked as we were. I didn't say a word. Charles looked at me and nodded his head. "I know," he said, "I'll never do anything like *that* again!"

University field supervisor Arthur Fredman advises:

Avoid a back-and-forth engagement with a student. Use nonconfrontational language. It's important that we listen to what a student is saying by rephrasing or paraphrasing, "Do you mean . . . ?" or, "Is this the way you want me to understand what happened?"

T.I.P.S.

A running record or checklist helps you plot the frequency and pattern of a behavior. Include the time, the students involved, and a description of the behavior or incident. An incident report form gives students a way to report and assume accountability for their actions. It is also helpful for keeping track of who did what to whom and allows you to quickly document the event with your own description.

Incident Report Form

(Form to be completed by students involved, with additional comments by the teacher.)

Student's name: _____ Date: _____

Teacher: _____ Date: _____

Circle one:

First report

Second report

(Continued)

(Continued)

Students involved:

_____

Where did the incident occur?

_____

In your own words, briefly describe what happened.

_____

_____

In your opinion, what do you think would be a fair action to be taken?

_____

Teacher's notes:

_____

_____

_____

_____

_____

_____

Chapter Five

Communicating

Miscommunication Happens

Young students frequently confuse or misuse *homonyms* or *words that sound alike.*

A second grader came in with her wrist in a cast and told the class, "My mother says I can't do any work because I hurt my *write* hand."

Hanna, Grade 4, gave this explanation in math class: "I keep my guinea pig in a shoebox, which is a rectangular *prison.*"

Here is a fact given during science class, Grade 5: "Insects must be pretty smart, because the book says you can classify them by their phylum or *genius.*"

According to one eight-year-old student, "A fraction is *abortion* [a portion] of something."

An upper grader heard me congratulate a teacher on achieving *tenure.* The boy said afterward, "She doesn't look bad for teaching *ten years.*"

Steven's father wrote to thank a first-year teacher for having a class discussion about steroids. The topic in science class was *asteroids.*

One rainy morning, I threw on my raincoat to meet my third graders at the door. As I hung up it up, I noticed that Robert was watching me with a thoughtful look. "I think I know why they call it a *drench coat,*" he said.

Misunderstanding can also result from a child's literal interpretation of the teacher's instructions. A few years ago, I taught a demonstration writing lesson to a group of first graders. Before the end of the session, I asked the children to go over their papers.

As I was collecting the papers, I was surprised to see that one little girl had printed her work in pencil and then had traced every letter with black crayon so that the print was illegible. As most of the class was still working, I pointed to the paper and whispered, "Samantha, what happened here?"

Samantha whispered back, "You said '*go over it.*'"

One of my student teachers asked the class to write *in complete sentences,* but even so, she received many papers that contained only fragments. One boy told her the reason: "You said to write *incomplete sentences.*"

A new teacher told me that she had given this compliment to a student following her oral report. "I noticed that you had very good *eye contact.*"

The girl responded, "That's funny. I don't even wear glasses!"

Nadia warned me on the first day of third grade, "I'm a *very* bad speller."

I asked her, "How can you possibly know that for sure? School has only just started!"

"I know," Nadia said with a sigh, "because my mother told me I spell by *ink-stink.*"

T.I.P.S.

Try these strategies for effective communication:

Use your natural voice with students. There is no need to exaggerate or separate syllables. Example: Please line up and walk *qui-et-ly* in the hall.

Use first and third person correctly. Example: It was the first day for a new boy in the third-grade class that I was visiting. Sometime during the morning, the teacher, Mrs. Turansky, began to have some difficulty with the class. "Please be quiet before Mrs. Turansky gets upset!" she warned. The new boy turned to the student next to him and whispered, "If we don't tell her, she'll never know!"

Listen to Yourself

Watch your speech habits: be aware of and try to correct repetitive habits such as throat clearing or using verbal fillers, such as *uh, you know, um, like,* and *right?*

Give courteous responses to students: show interest with eye contact, nodding, and short verbal acknowledgements.

Address students respectfully: avoid, for instance, addressing the class as "you guys."

Pay attention to your tone: be pleasant, not condescending, annoyed, or sarcastic.

Avoid singling out a student.

"When Tommy is ready, we can all line up. Will someone please help Tommy put his things away? We're still waiting for you, Tommy. Tommy, did you hear me?"

Supply answers, when needed, and keep it short.

Teachers can provide a word list or word bank, or refer to the context, supply a synonym, or a give a clue to word meaning. A question is not an invitation for a long explanation.
"The Sahara is *arid,* which is another word for *dry.*"

Avoid verbal interruptions.

When students are so engrossed in their work that the room is practically silent, the teacher should not use the opportunity to make announcements.

Check your spelling.

A teacher gave these three extra words to her advanced spellers: optometrist, optician, and *optholmologist.*
The next day, the teacher received a note from a girl's father who thanked the teacher for giving the additional words. It was signed, "Becky's dad, the *ophthalmologist."*

MEETING THE PARENTS

Parent night or back-to-school night are times for parents to meet the teacher and find out about the instructional program, goals for the year, and your general requirements. Most of all, parents need to be reassured that their child is in good hands: happy, safe, and learning.
You can prepare a handout, have the students write notes for their parents to answer, and display samples of the students' work. Greet the parents, but avoid becoming involved in long conversations or "conferences." Keep your remarks short, and give parents specific ways that they can help their child at home.

As I was a midyear hire, my first back-to-school night came in October of my second year of teaching. While we were straightening up the classroom, I told my students that I was looking forward to meeting their parents and working together for a pleasant and productive year. One of the boys said matter-of-factly, "My dad just wants to see what you look like."

By seven o'clock that evening, I felt that everything was going well. Parents had wandered around the room, admired the projects, and were sitting at their children's desks, waiting expectantly to hear my presentation. About halfway through my talk, a parent looked at his watch, got up, and walked out. Embarrassed because I thought that I had gone on too long, I quickly wrapped up my speech. Later in the evening, the same parent stopped me in the hall and told me why he had left so abruptly. "Your talk was so interesting," he said, "that I didn't realize that my son is not in your class."

THE PARENT CONFERENCE

This is a meeting to share the students' progress with their parents. It's also a time to address concerns and make suggestions for improvement. Strategies for a successful conference follow.

- Adhere closely to the conference schedule. A parent should not be kept waiting.
- Put the parent at ease with a comment about the student's strengths and talents.
- Sit next to or near parents, rather than directly across from them.
- Make sure that the information and work samples you are showing belong to the student you are discussing.
- Use appropriate terms when discussing academics, such as *skill building, learning to apply, practicing,* and *needs to strengthen.*
- Have some items such as toys, crayons, and paper on hand to keep siblings occupied.
- Have paper ready to record issues that the parent raises or for the parent to take down some of your suggestions.
- Listen closely to what parents have to say.
- Everything discussed at a parent-teacher conference is *strictly confidential.*

CHAPTER SIX

Instructing

FORMULATING CLEAR OBJECTIVES AND A PLAN

Too often, the purpose of a lesson is vague or unstated, leaving it to the students to make connections to previous skills. Clear objectives focus learning on the future—what the student will be able to do by the end of the lesson or series of lessons. Also, objectives can be used as measures of mastery, showing how far we've progressed.

Objectives need only to be attainable and straightforward. They can be stated or written in a few words and a few minutes.

For example:

To count by 5s to 100

To circle the past-tense verbs in a paragraph

Use clear key words, such as the ones in the column at the left.

Clear Objectives (Use)	*Cloudy Objectives (Avoid)*
Classify	Remember
Compare	Develop
Recite	Recall
Draw	Analyze
Underline	Understand
Highlight	Realize
Act out	Know
Design	Plan
Construct	Memorize

Illustrate	Find out
Label	Learn
Select	Think about
Identify	Appreciate

Whether teaching someone a beautiful backhand or how to find the volume of a cylinder, skill acquisition follows the same steps. Learning begins with the *foundation,* or basics. *Scaffolding* is a term that refers to building upon foundation skills.

First, set an attainable goal. Demonstrate and break down the skill into smaller elements. Explain and show the steps slowly and clearly. Vary the approach if necessary. Give the student time to practice each element. Provide individual instruction. Listen and respond to the learner's questions, and reteach parts of the skill if needed.

DIFFERENTIATING INSTRUCTION

You'll find that your students have different learning styles. Some students are visual learners while others learn better through listening (auditory) or by touch (tactile). Some students learn better by imitation, others by repetition, and still others by trial and error. Children read and write at different speeds. Your students are at different maturity levels. In addition, you may have students with identified learning disabilities or others who are English language learners (ELL). The challenge is to provide for all of the different needs in your class.

T.I.P.S.

There are specific ways to provide for each student's instructional needs:

Design centers and activities to be suitable for students at all levels. Classroom libraries should contain fiction and nonfiction books that cover a wide variety of reading levels. A multisensory approach to teaching works well for all learning preferences.

You can group students according to specific academic needs or mix ability levels to provide cooperative learning. Keep groups flexible, and provide enrichment for students who have mastered concepts and skills.

The advanced students in your class also have academic needs, and may be particularly gifted. Some districts have criteria for entrance into gifted and talented programs.

Sometimes children become nervous, as in the case of a six-year-old child who looked up while reading a basic list of sight words and said, "I want you to know that I have *test anxiety*."

Resist the temptation of having advanced students help you correct papers or instruct other children. Instead, you can provide research opportunities, leadership roles, and projects that highlight the students' interests. These not only increase motivation but also help build self-confidence and pride.

Students' work can be published. The Anthology of Poetry, for example, produces a professionally bound hardcover book. Its mission is to encourage young writers (Anthology of Poetry, 2008).

Even young children can research, interview, and write articles for their own newsletter or class newspaper. This type of project creates interesting and purposeful class work and homework, and it results in a published format for the class, the school, and for parents. A newsletter provides a way for students to write about topics that appeal to them.

Basic Lesson Plan

Objective

Materials

Procedure

Follow-up

Expanded Lesson Plan

Objective

Materials

Procedure

Motivation

Group practice

Individual practice

Closure

Follow-up

Homework, enrichment, reinforcement

Review, Review, Review . . .

In the beginning, I thought that my students would grasp a skill or concept the moment that I taught it. I was surprised and disappointed when there seemed to be pieces missing. My fifth graders would stare at me blankly when I referred to the same subject matter we had covered only a week earlier. "We never had that," they'd say. "You never taught us that."

Carl, my friend and mentor, understood. "It's the *never* part that bothers us," he told me, and added that teaching and learning works like this: Take three steps forward, a step backward, and then another three steps forward. Accept that your students need a review of the material, even though it *seems* as if they caught it the first time around. A good strategy is to start every lesson with a short review to refresh everyone's memory. Have your students initiate the review, or use a practice quiz or some math examples as a warm-up.

Motivating

While no one can *make* another person learn, you can motivate a person to *want* to learn. Many teachers bring their own passions and talents into interesting lessons that connect to the curriculum. Travel experiences, yoga, robotics, African drumming, singing, sewing, calligraphy, Irish dancing, sketching, juggling, origami, playwriting, photography, and puppetry are only some of the teacher specialties.

Motivation can also come from a change in the usual *lesson format*. Consider starting lessons with an intriguing question or by showing an object or picture that relates to the topic. Lessons can be introduced with a story, music, or poem. Motivation also works with a change in *materials*. For example, free resources, such as train schedules, catalogs, travel brochures, and museum booklets, become the basis for interesting and realistic math problems.

You can change the *location* of the lesson. Find out if you can take your class to the gym, auditorium, or outside for a lesson. Within the classroom, create a makeshift podium, make signs that read "pro" and "con" or "for" and "against," and move desks to set up a debate or panel discussion. Changing the *role* of the students also works well. For example, upper-grade students can read with younger ones.

You can also change the *participants*. For example, team up with a teacher at another grade level to spark new interest in a lesson. Just be sure not to fall prey to a predictable pattern that takes the place of teaching, such as showing a video every Friday afternoon.

Desk Arrangements and Advantages

Columns and rows facing front: This conventional desk arrangement is useful for testing, first arrangement for the year to address students, and to learn names and faces.

Pairs: This arrangement works well when students are quietly working or reading with a partner.

Groups of four: This square arrangement is suitable for group or project work where each group member has a job.

Lines of six or more facing each other: This is a practical arrangement for whole-class discussions.

Circle or semicircle: This desk arrangement promotes sharing ideas, brainstorming, and solving problems.

T.I.P.S.

We want our students to be inquisitive and to ask questions. We would like our students to be self-sufficient and seek answers through research. But first, we need to know what motivates children to learn.

Demonstrations: Children enjoy watching exhibitions of skills and demonstrating skills of their own.

Extremes: Very large or very small numbers, record breaking, or unusual facts all capture students' attention.

Objects: Children enjoy handling strange or unusual objects.

Animals: The more peculiar, the more fascinated children become.

Stories: Students are captivated by stories with suspense, surprise, or interesting characters.

(Continued)

(Continued)

Events, biographies, and situations: Children are motivated to learn about things that relate directly to their own lives.

Humor: Children find many things funny—slapstick, anything silly, unexpected, futuristic, imaginary, or unusual (words, odors, voices, names, or sounds).

Reversals: Students are fascinated by changing roles (child as teacher) or changes in time ("if you lived in colonial days...").

Variation of visuals: You can keep students interested with a changing-weather chart or globe.

Change in method: Give students a variety of assignments, such as fill-in-the-blank, highlight, circle, graph, sketch, or label (e.g., the parts of a volcano).

Intriguing questions: Keep students interested by asking questions such as, "Who do you think the child is in this picture? What do you think she is doing? What will happen next? How do you know?"

"TAKE OUT YOUR HOMEWORK"

This seemingly innocuous request can give even the most confident among us a twinge. Surprisingly, concerns about homework are something students and teachers share.

The Student's Viewpoint

"The assignments are too long, (too boring, too hard). I'd rather play or watch TV. The worst part of homework is that I have to do it after school, *during my free time!*"

The Teacher's Viewpoint

"Homework is necessary. Students need to practice the skills I've taught. It also provides review. It's difficult to gear the homework to all of the different levels of the students. Also, I have to deal with excuses for forgotten homework, incomplete homework, and homework that is not handed in at all. I feel frustrated when the parents don't supervise or take an interest. Often, I have to check or grade assignments *during my free time!*"

T.I.P.S.

- Never use homework as a punishment.
- Make an effort to keep assignments interesting and relevant.
- Remind students to take home all of the materials they need to complete the work.
- Keep a record of the homework assignments you give.
- Check all homework assignments. Record incomplete or missing assignments.
- Alert the parents if homework is not completed.
- Find out the school's policy on assigning homework on weekends and holidays.

Notes

CHAPTER SEVEN

Observing and Being Observed

Confident teachers feel secure in their knowledge of the subject matter and presentation methods. They are consistent and fair in their decision making. Confident teachers are not defensive or concerned about making an impression. Rather, they are approachable and view visits from administrators as opportunities to share their class accomplishments.

T.I.P.S.
A positive attitude begins with an understanding of what administrators and supervisors are looking for and how you can put you, your students, and your visitors at ease.

BE YOURSELF . . . AND BE PREPARED

Give a brief description of what the observer is about to see, and supply your visitor with an outline, textbook, or materials that accompany the lesson. Ask if the observer would like to be introduced to the class or participate in some way. Make sure the purpose or the objective of the lesson is clear to everyone, circulate, and keep an eye on the time. A valuable idea is to have the plan visible on a chart or board. This way, you, the visitor, and your class will stay on track throughout the lesson. It will also help you plan your time.

Visitations serve a variety of purposes. For example, an administrator or supervisor may need to come in at a scheduled or unscheduled time to do a *formal observation*. During this time, the observer may *script* the lesson, or record what you say. The clarity of the lesson is important with regard to its basic elements: objectives, motivation, procedure, practice, closure, and follow-up. Ideally, a discussion of the observation will take place on the same day or soon after. In any event, it's always a good idea to keep a copy of the lesson plan. You can refer to the following general list of checkpoints as a guide for preparing.

- Neatness: clean closets, lockers, and desks.
- Preparation: materials ready with agenda visible.
- Motivation: method for focusing students implemented at the beginning of the lesson.
- Objective: clearly stated or written.
- Feedback: circulates around room, uses effective questioning techniques, encourages student participation, waits for students to answer, and gives positive reinforcement.
- Knowledge of subject: vocabulary, concepts and skills broken down or explained.
- Evidence of learning: work posted, projects displayed.
- Management skills: calm, quick, quiet methods of keeping students focused.
- Communication: appropriate tone and voice, with good eye contact.

There will be times when a staff member may need to observe the behavior of a student. Parents or volunteers may come in to help with a project, activity or special event, or they may accompany you on a field trip. Visitors from colleges may be assigned to visit your classroom. Any of these can be considered forms of observing, so be aware that regardless of how short the stay, visitors receive a sense of how well you handle your group.

LEARNING BY OBSERVING

My first classroom visitation taught me the most because it was by far the worst.

My best friend in college was Ginny, and we were thrilled to have received the same school assignment. We assumed that *observe* meant to passively watch, as in "watch a movie," and we expected to be entertained, which turned out to be our biggest mistake.

Ginny and I drove to an inner-city school to observe a sixth-grade language arts class of more than 30 students; from the start, we got the impression that the teacher wasn't in the mood for unexpected visitors on a Monday morning. We were told to sit in the back while the students struggled, one by one, to read articles aloud from the newspaper.

We figured out why the class was so quiet. The articles were uncensored by the teacher, so virtually all of them contained explicit descriptions of accidents or attacks.

The teacher hunched over her desk, scribbled in her notebook, and occasionally supplied a word for the reader without even looking up, "Wrecked. Hospitalized. Serious." The droning went on for almost an hour. The room was hot, and I was getting giddy from trying to avoid eye contact with Ginny, who kept looking at her watch. Also, I could hear her stomach growling.

She finally whispered to me, "When this is over, can we *please* go to lunch?" Silence replaced the reader's voice.

The teacher stood up, and with hands on hips used a sharp tone that made everyone in the room jump. "I would expect the visitors in the back to be quiet and show some *respect!*" The students twisted around in their seats to stare at us.

We had been reprimanded as if we were students in her class, and although we were embarrassed, Ginny and I came away with valuable lessons about teacher *and* visitor responsibilities. The impression of that visit would always stay with me. I learned to set standards for visitors and correct the individuals privately if something precipitated a problem.

The following section lists actual behaviors of classroom visitors.

Dos and Don'ts of Observing

- Do be punctual—do not check the time obviously or repeatedly.
- Do turn off your phone—do not check messages or send text messages.
- Do use mouthwash—do not chew gum.
- Do dress appropriately—do not wear jeans or extra tight or sheer clothing.

- Do observe courteously—do not attract negative attention by doodling, humming, tapping, talking, or whispering during the lesson.
- Do offer to participate—do not correct or help students unless invited to do so by the teacher.
- Do bathe and use lotion or powder—do not wear perfume or strong cologne or aftershave.
- Do have a good breakfast—do not carry a container or cup of coffee or tea with you.
- Do bring a lunch that is well wrapped—do not bring food with a detectable odor.
- Do keep a water bottle or juice in a bag—do not carry the bottle in full view or drink it in class.
- Do ask to take notes—do not write anything that you would not want the teacher to read.
- Do compliment students—do not give candy or rewards.
- Do come in organized—do not clean out your wallet, purse, or bag during class.
- Do use the faculty restroom—do not take care of personal hygiene, such as nail filing, applying lipstick or lip balm, or taking medication during class.
- Do keep the teacher's and students' names confidential—do not share the students' names or photos with anyone outside the school.
- Do document your visit—do not leave the information to memory.

CHAPTER EIGHT

Respecting

PROVIDING FOR DIFFERENCES AND DISABILITIES

Get to know your class one student at a time. When working with a class, there is a tendency to think in terms of the whole group rather than individuals. I encourage student teachers to listen, as it's the best way to learn about your students. Students' comments, such as, "Tomorrow my grandmother is coming from Brazil" or, "My mother is going to have more time for me because she just quit her job" can be illuminating.

You can expect a wide range of intellectual and physical abilities as well as various stages of social and emotional maturity. You will be informed about children with special education classifications who may need accommodations in the regular classroom.

William Gaventa (2008), M. Div., associate professor and director, Community and Congregational Supports at The Elizabeth M. Boggs Center on Developmental Disabilities, UMDNJ-Robert Wood Johnson Medical School in New Brunswick, New Jersey, gives this insight into the needs of individuals with autism: "People may communicate very differently, as well as be at any different place on the spectrum. Predictability and routines are often very important for safety, security, and a sense of control" (pp. 30–31).

T.I.P.S.

There may be students in your class who have difficulty with learning, listening, communicating, or remembering, so it's important to be aware of behaviors that repeat, follow a pattern, or interfere with the child's academic functioning in the class.

Examples of challenges that may need to be addressed:

- small motor difficulties
- short attention span
- emotional outbursts
- difficulty putting thoughts into words
- speech or language issues
- low frustration threshold
- impulsive behavior
- difficulty socializing
- hyperactivity or inability to sit still or concentrate
- reticence or detachment
- visual or perceptual difficulties
- difficulty organizing

CULTURAL DIVERSITY AND YOUR ENGLISH LANGUAGE LEARNERS

Situation A

Pick a foreign country—any country. Now, imagine that you are a new student, sitting silently hour after hour, in a classroom. You are unable to understand or make yourself understood. Students and teachers talk loudly at you with a great deal of gesturing and exaggerating, but all you can do is shake your head or shrug to indicate that all of it is lost on you.

Everyone in your class knows the routine. You follow and imitate. You want to tell them, "In my old school, I was a leader, at the top of my class." You wish you could tell them about the art award you won last year. You have always loved to draw. At the end of the day, you can't wait to get home to familiar territory. Your family knows that you are unhappy, but there is little anyone can do for you. The weeks stretch out in front of you.

Situation B

You are in the same class in the foreign country. You are given a warm welcome and a desk near the teacher. Your name is on it in English.

One of the students shows you how to find the office and the restrooms. Another student helps you match pictures of everyday objects with words on cards.

The teacher shows everyone your country on the big wall map. You draw a picture of your family, and the teacher smiles and holds it up.

Each student says, "Hi, my name is . . ." and holds up a name card. Even the teacher tries to say a few words in your language to show the class how difficult learning a new language can be. It doesn't matter that she makes mistakes because everyone laughs, including the teacher! A group of children sits with you at lunchtime. Your smile shows your thanks to the teacher for making you feel welcome and unafraid on your first day.

T.I.P.S.

Make your classroom a welcoming place.

There are many ways that you can make a new student feel at home. Help your students to decorate with flags of many nations. Show the flag of the United Nations and discuss the dove and olive branch as a symbol of peace. You can find the new student's country of origin on the map and globe and tell about their monetary system, foods, and customs. The new student can teach your students some new words and phrases.

A good book to read and discuss with students of all ages is *Molly's Pilgrim* (Cohen, 1988). You might also introduce Emma Lazarus's (1883/n.d.) poem "The New Colossus."

Involve your class in setting up an area for the new student and making arrangements for helping the new student become acclimated.

Provide plenty of interesting materials. ELL students can feel lost in the midst of a busy classroom. The English as a second language (ESL) teacher can provide workbooks or suggest activities, such as flashcards of common objects and their names, to do with another student. Start or provide a picture and word dictionary for the student. You can find out if there are other students or teachers in the school who are able to translate, as there are times that it becomes truly necessary to communicate. I remember the year that I had three well-worn bilingual dictionaries on my desk—Japanese, Russian, and Korean.

The areas of music, art, and sports may provide natural outlets for the student who speaks no or little English. For example, in the same fifth-grade class, Suki surprised everyone with her ability to draw, while Armand distinguished himself on the soccer field.

The following practical advice is from Jory Oulhiad, a doctoral student in curriculum and instruction for culturally and linguistically diverse learners at Kansas State University and an experienced teacher of ELL.

- Speak slowly and clearly (not loudly).
- Use visuals, such as diagrams, maps, pictures, and photos.
- Label everyday objects.
- Allow the student to use a bilingual dictionary, or ask a classmate who speaks the same language to translate. ELLs need a way to make themselves understood.
- Be conscious of your use of idioms, and explain their meanings.
- Provide opportunities for students to work cooperatively, since socialization is an important part of language acquisition.
- Use this opportunity to teach your class about ways in which people are alike and different, and the richness it adds to the school and community.
- Be patient. You'll be surprised at how fast and how much your new student will absorb!
- See that your ELL students are on time for their ELL classes. Ask how you can follow up.

TEACHING VALUES

Show your students that their classroom functions like a community by setting clear rules together. Show students and let them practice using acceptable social behavior, resisting peer pressure, and making good decisions through role-playing situations.

T.I.P.S.

Sample ELL Student-Performance Checklist

Student: _____ Teacher: _____ Date: _____

Date entered: _____ L1 (first language): _____

Student knows:

Common school objects: *pencil, desk, pen, paper*

Hi, Good morning

My name is

Please

Thank you

Goodbye

I like

I don't like

I need

I don't understand

Student can:

Use numbers to count

Tell birthday

Tell address

Recall telephone number

Identify colors

Name days of the week

Describe feelings: *happy, sad, hungry, tired, sick*

Identify parts of the body

Name common foods: *milk, bread*

Identify common animals: *dog, cat, bird, fish*

T.I.P.S.

Set the tone for the day with an interactive group meeting to make announcements, share news, or engage in a group activity.

Show appreciation: be generous with your thanks, and suggest ways for children to show theirs.

Be a role model: show students that *you* care about others and that together you can help others. Make cards for children in hospitals, or tackle a cause or issue that the students feel strongly about.

Practice kind acts: demonstrate holding the door, taking turns, and waiting in line.

Post visual reminders: have students make posters to illustrate good values.

Invite special speakers: your school may have programs that highlight character education, or you might suggest someone you know who is an outstanding speaker.

Teach students to respect education: you might use quotes from successful people to show how they felt about education. An example is this quotation from the 14th-century philosopher Erasmus: "Whenever I have a little money I buy books, and if anything is left over I buy food and clothes" (Galli & Olsen, 2000, p. 342).

A List of Values . . .

The following is a list of topics for discussion, skits, posters, stories, or problem-solving activities.

- Self-control: knowing what the boundaries are, and staying within them.
- Patience: waiting for something or someone.
- Thoughtfulness: thinking and doing for others.
- Obedience: following rules, regulations, and laws.
- Honesty: practicing truthfulness.
- Punctuality: being on time.

- Determination: not giving up.
- Empathy: understanding how another person feels.
- Appreciation: giving thanks and showing gratitude.
- Confidence: feeling that you can do something.
- Respect: having a high regard for someone.
- Humility: not bragging about your accomplishments.
- Kindness: showing a friendly attitude toward others.
- Forgiveness: not holding an action or words against someone.
- Optimism: looking at the bright side.

Notes

CHAPTER NINE

Reflecting

SELF-ASSESSMENT: A SIGN
OF PROFESSIONAL GROWTH

These first years are the cornerstone of your career. At this point, you cannot imagine or predict the power of your words or the extent of your influence, but it's important to realize that the teaching profession comes with great obligations.

As you develop a style of your own and strategies that work, you owe it to your students to ask yourself, "What worked well? What do I need to do better? What other approaches can I try?"

Teachers and coaches give gifts without expecting to be praised or even remembered, but our impact can be remarkable, as this story by Edward Warshow, a former high school English teacher, shows.

"I went to a retired teacher's luncheon recently, and a woman came up to me, introduced herself, and said, 'I was your student teacher!'"

She still remembered how she had begun her career in Mr. Warshow's senior English class. She recalled that after a few weeks of observing, Ed had told her that she would teach a lesson the following week. But when the day came, she had become too nervous.

"I can't go on," she had told him. She expected Ed to insist that she teach the class. Instead he told her, "So? You don't have to teach today. You can tell me when you feel ready." And the very next day she taught the class.

After so many years, Ed remembered the event, too.

"You know, if I had insisted, I would have discouraged her from having a long and wonderful career. What's the difference in waiting until she felt she could do it? In fact, she became a sterling and very popular teacher. I should know . . . I was her department chairman for eleven years!"

We all get caught up in teaching for the moment, especially when testing drives instruction. An emphasis on student achievement creates a sense of urgency to complete the material in the textbook and to cover the skills in preparation for the standardized tests. In some places, teacher performance is judged by the results of those tests. Other districts give incentives such as merit pay, "master teacher" status, or similar rewards for outstanding teaching. The danger is that teachers can transfer their goal-oriented concerns to their students with an overemphasis on test preparation, so it's important that the teacher keep a level head and provide a balanced educational program.

In addition, it seems to me that jealousy, envy, and competition weakens the very nature of teaching and learning. From the creative bulletin board next to yours, to the teacher whose class always has the best attendance, to the class with the highest test scores, try to compliment, not compete or compare. Seize opportunities to applaud your students for doing their best.

T.I.P.S.

Follow these steps on the ladder for successful teaching:

- Keep it interesting.
- Keep it simple.
- Keep it big.
- Keep it bold.
- Keep it visible.
- *Keep it real.*

Now that you are a part of the cycle, you can begin your own compilation of wisdom and witticism in a class of your own. You will develop successful strategies and apply them to new situations. You will weed out advice that does not help and add your own touch to advice that does.

You will have many mentors and you will, when the time comes, mentor others. In the meantime, use your authority wisely, and treat your students as you would like to be treated. It won't be long until you receive one of the many immeasurable rewards of this profession . . . a note like this one, written all wobbly and misspelled:

"Dear techer, thank you very plenty."

Notes

References and
Additional Resources

Anthology of Poetry. (2008). *Anthology of poetry.* Retrieved March 16, 2010, from http://www.anthologyofpoetry.com/pages/index.cfm.

Baer, D., & Samkoff, R. (2008, March). Local government and student government working together . . . it's elementary! *New Jersey Municipalities Magazine,* 46–48.

Cohen, B. (1998). *Molly's pilgrim.* New York: Lothrop, Lee & Shepard Books.

Cullum, A. (2000). *The geranium on the windowsill just died, but teacher you went right on.* New York: Harlin Quist Books.

Gaventa, W. (2008, May). "Of course"—ministry and service by adults with autism. *Autism and Faith: A Journey Into Community,* 30–31.

Galli, M., & Olsen, T. (Eds.). (2000). *121 Christians everyone should know.* Nashville, TN: Christianity Today.

Goetzel, R. (2005). *Examining the value of integrating occupational health and safety programs in the workplace.* Washington, DC: National Institute of Occupational Safety and Health (NIOSH).

Lazarus. E. (n.d.). The new colossus. *Poemhunter.com.* Retrieved March 16, 2010, from http://www.poemhunter.com/poem/the-new-colossus/. (Original work published 1883)

Nichols, G. (Ed.). (2009). *Anthology of poetry.* Asheboro, NC: Anthology of Poetry.

Samkoff, R. (2001, November 18). Assignment of inclusion. *The New York Times,* 14NJ1.

ThinkExist.com. (1999–2010). Franklin D. Roosevelt Quotes. *ThinkExist.com.* Retrieved March 16, 2010, from http://thinkexist.com/quotes/franklin_d._roosevelt/3.html.

QUALITY WEB SITES FOR TEACHERS

URL	Topic
www.brainpop.com	Practice activities in math, language arts
www.mathplayground.com	Practice activities in math for K–6
www.english-4kids.com	Clever ELL activities and worksheets
www.manythings.org	Interesting ELL activities and worksheets
www.teachingheart.net	Lesson plans and Web sites for K–6 teachers, comprehensive
www.teachernet.com	Lesson plans and activities for K–8
www.themailbox.com	Well-designed, practical learning activities and classroom ideas for all subject areas
www.pbskids.org	Read-aloud, read-along stories
www.ajkids.com	Ask Jeeves activities and flashcards in math
www.kidsinfo.com	Excellent links to teacher Web sites and lesson plans
www.nationalgeographic.com/kids	Amazing facts, creative writing
www.aplusmath.com	Good math site for students under age 8, games and flashcards
www.atozteacherstuff.com	Useful worksheets, themes, printables, lessons, and tips for K–6 teachers

Index

Appearance, 6
Arrangements, desk, 43–44

Balance, 27
Behavior problems, 13–14, 30–32,
        33–34 (box)

Calendars, school, 6
Charts, instructional, 19
Classroom
    desk arrangements, 43–44
    management, 15–16
    space use, 22
Clear objectives, 39–40
Cliques, 16
Cloudy objectives, 39–40
Communicating
    at back to school nights, 37–38
    by listening to oneself, 36–37
    mis-, 35–36
Community connections, 9
Conferences, 14, 38
Content, 27
Creativity, 16
Cultural diversity, 52–54

Dantus, Larry, 28
Desk arrangements, 43–44
Differences, 51
Differentiating instruction,
        40–41 (box)
Disabilities, 51

Discipline, 13
Diversity, cultural, 52–54

English Language Learners (ELL),
        52–54, 55 (box)
Enrichment, 21, 27, 40–41 (box)
Exercise and productivity, 28–29

Favoritism, 13
Ford, Ginny, 49
Formal observations, 48
Fredman, Art, 6

Gaventa, William, 51
Giventer, Evelyn, 21
Goetzel, Ron, 28
Grading errors, 12
Graphics, 19
Groups, managing, 27–28

Hall passes, 12
Health and safety, 22–25
Homework, 44, 45 (box)
Homonyms, 35
Humor, 6

Incident report forms, 33–34 (box)
Information sheets, 5 (box)
Instructing/instruction
    differentiating, 40–41 (box)
    formulating clear objectives and
        plans for, 39–40

motivating during, 42–44
  review in, 42
Instructional charts, 19
Interruptions, 14–15

Klein, Harold M., 9

Lazarus, Emma, 53
Lesson planning, 12–13, 29
  creative, 16
  differentiating instruction and,
    40–41 (box)
  motivation and, 42–44
  review and, 42
Lost and found, 17 (box)

Managing
  behavior issues, 13–14, 30–32,
    33–34 (box)
  classroom, 15–16
  groups, 27–28
  paperwork, 29–30
  planning, 29
  productivity, 28–29
Materials, teaching, 6, 19
  purposeful projects and, 21–22
  storage, 19–20, 21 (box)
Messages, delivery of, 11
Misbehavior. See Behavior
Miscommunication, 35–36
Mistakes, 11–14
Molly's Pilgrim, 53
Motivation, 17, 42–44

Names, students', 12
Nonconfrontational language, 33 (box)

Objectives, clear, 39–40
Observation
  formal, 48
  learning by, 48–50
  of teachers by others, 47–48
Office work, 19
Organizing, 19–25
Oulhiad, Jory, 54

Pace, 27
Paperwork, 12, 29–30

Parents, 37–38
  observation by, 48
Pictures, 19
Plan books, 6
Planning, 12–13, 29
  formulating clear objectives and,
    39–40
Plotnikov, Dimitriy, 28
Principals, 8, 15, 16
Productivity and exercise, 28–29
Projects, purposeful, 21–22
Purposeful projects, 21–22

Relationships, work, 6
Reminders, daily, 12 (box)
Respect, 15
  of cultural diversity, 52–54
  of differences and disabilities, 51
  teaching values and, 54–57
Resume, 4
Retrieval and storage systems, 19–20,
  21 (box)
Review, 42
Rewards, 12
Role, teachers', 6–7
Roosevelt, Franklin D., 31
Running record, 33 (box)

Safety and health, 22–25
Scaffolding, 40
Schades, Judith, 21
Self-assessment, 59–61
Sense of humor, 6
Sick days, 15
Sound, 28
Space, wise use of, 22
Storage and retrieval systems, 19–20,
  21 (box)
Stretch breaks, 28
Students
  behavior problems in, 13–14
  cliques among, 16
  conferences with, 14
  delivering messages to, 11
  English Language Learner (ELL),
    52–54, 55 (box)
  enrichment, 21, 27, 40–41 (box)
  guessing about, 12

hall passes for, 12
homework, 44, 45 (box)
lost and found for possessions of,
    17 (box)
misbehavior by, 13
motivating, 17, 42–44
names, 12
respect of, 15
Substitutes, 29
Supervisors, 6, 15, 16

Teachers
bond between, 3
conferences, 14, 38
defining role of, 6–7
illness in, 15
keeping sense of humor intact, 6
learning by observation, 48–50
listening to themselves, 36–37
meeting parents, 37–38
observation of, 47–48

off duty time, 7 (box)
preparation for teaching,
    4–6
questions from new, 14–17
self-assessment by, 59–61
taking care of oneself before taking
    care of others, 4–6
work relationships, 8
Teaching
defined, 1–2
general principles of, 3–4
materials, 6, 19
values, 54–57
Time management, 12–13, 14–15
Timing, 28

Values, 54–57
Voice, 27

Work relationships, 8
Worksheets, 19

CORWIN

A SAGE Company

The Corwin logo—a raven striding across an open book—represents the union of courage and learning. Corwin is committed to improving education for all learners by publishing books and other professional development resources for those serving the field of PreK–12 education. By providing practical, hands-on materials, Corwin continues to carry out the promise of its motto: **"Helping Educators Do Their Work Better."**